WITH GOD'S HELP...
YES, I CAN!

Life Lessons
from Philippians 4

Dr. William (Bill) A. Snow, Jr.

Praise for *With God's Help... Yes, I Can!*

Dr. William (Bill) Snow is the very epitome of the "Yes, I Can" spirit. I have known Bill over 45 years. I first met him when my family moved into the same subdivision as Bill's family. He was a teen when he gave his life to Christ. He attended Wesley College, where he accepted the call into the ministry and married his wife Myra.

Shortly after graduation, Bill and Myra moved to Anniston, Alabama, to pastor Edgewood Church. Under the leadership of the Holy Spirit, Bill and Myra saw the small church grow. A real "Can Do" moment came when the church relocated to its current location. There the church continued to grow and expand through the addition of a new building with a gymnasium, a children's wing, and new Sunday school classes. The church also extended the parking lot and added new staff. Throughout this expansion, which can be a difficult time for any church, Bill, through God's help, lead Edgewood through continued growth in numbers and spirit.

I challenge you, as you read the book, to look up, let go, and adopt the "I Can" spirit that Bill is writing about. With the help and guidance of the Holy Spirit, you can accomplish what God has planned for you.

—Dr. Tommy Chapman
Pastor, neighbor, counselor and friend

Dr. Bill Snow has been a friend of mine for almost ten years. Not only is Dr. Snow a friend of mine, but I work with him as associate pastor of Edgewood Church. Bill is totally committed to Jesus Christ, not only on Sundays, but 24/7. Bill is committed not only to the church, but to his beautiful wife, Myra, his precious daughters, sons-in-law, and, of course, his grandkids. I have watched him handle good and difficult situations, and always Jesus has been glorified. Over the years, as I have become more acquainted in the community, people would ask who I am, where I work, and without my saying another word, they would mention the name Bill Snow. Everyone always speaks highly of Bill. I thank the Lord that in the fourth-quarter years of my life, I have had the privilege of walking beside my best friend, Dr. Bill Snow.

—Rev. Barry Thompson
Associate Pastor, Edgewood Church

Working with Bill Snow on this project has been a wonderful experience. He is one of the most genuine men I have ever known, and this book reflects that. He not only believes what he writes, but he lives it. I am honored to call him friend and to have had a small part in the production of this book. It is a testimony to what one can do with God's help.

—Donna Shivers
Volunteer and Special Friend

ISBN: 978-1-946730-17-6 (paperback)
ISBN: 978-1-946730-18-3 (hardcover)
ISBN: 978-1-946730-19-0 (e-book)

Edited by Jennifer Harshman, HarshmanServices.com

Cover and Book Design by James Woosley, FreeAgentPress.com

Cover created from photos by:
    Rachel Cook (https://unsplash.com/@grafixgurl247) and
    Alfred Aloushy (https://unsplash.com/@musickid98)

Published by Free Agent Press
FreeAgentPress.com
Satsuma, Alabama 36572
VID: 20211114

*This book is dedicated to the
most important person in my life—
My wife Myra.*

*We met at a wedding (not ours) over 40 years ago.
For me, it was love at first sight! She's a blue-eyed blonde
that sang like a bird and looked like a queen.
I was immediately smitten . . . and still am.*

*She loves Jesus. He's all she's ever known.
She was saved young, and she's still going strong for God.
She's my Proverbs 31 woman. Her smile, her wit, and her
laughter light up a room. Myra, you are my best friend.*

*We started out as children, it seems now as we are
much older, wiser, and grown-up (grandparents). I have
learned from you (am still learning) to enjoy the sunset,
a cup of coffee, and to stop and smell the roses.
It is my honor to do life with you. Thank you.*

CONTENTS

PREFACE

History tells us that Nero was the Emperor of Rome from 54–68 AD. In the beginning of his reign, he was a good ruler; however, things changed when Rome burned in 64 AD. Nero blamed Christians and began killing them, causing him to become a terrible and cruel ruler. It is during Nero's reign that Paul is imprisoned and writes this letter to the Christians at Philippi. This letter is an attempt by Paul to clean up issues within the church that could be negative, harmful, and hurtful, such as division among believers, false teachers, and pessimism over his imprisonment. It is in this environment that he reminds the church to have joy in their lives, and he thanks them for their faith. Paul boldly lives what he writes—that he can do all things through Christ who strengthens him.

FOREWORD

Napoleon Bonaparte said it best: "Leaders are dealers in hope." If there has ever been a time in which people need hope and encouragement, I believe it is today. My dear friend, Dr. Bill Snow, has written a book that will give hope to everyone who reads it.

I am convinced that one of the enemy's greatest weapons is discouragement. His objective is simply to take away our courage. But I am so happy to report that we serve a God who continually exhorts us to be strong and courageous! *With God's Help... Yes, I Can* is a book that teaches practical ways to maintain the strength and courage that God provides for each of His children. This book teaches that God is for you, and He has a wonderful purpose for your life. Each chapter will challenge you to believe this simple truth—with God, all things are possible.

It was a great day in my life when I realized that the principles I live by will determine the world I live in. The principles in this book will help you grow in your Christian walk and become greatly encouraged in all that God wants to do in your life.

My advice to you is this: Warning—this book has the potential to change your life! It is certainly a page-turner. I was unable to put it down, and I believe that will be true for you as well.

Dig in and discover all God has in store for you!

Dr. Benny Tate
Senior Pastor of Rock Spring Church

ACKNOWLEDGMENTS

First and foremost:

To Donna Shivers for the words of encouragement for me to write a book. You believed in me before I believed in myself. Your countless hours correcting, reading, typing, sharing ideas, and rereading the manuscript were invaluable to me to finish this book. Your suggestions and thoughts were indispensable and essential to the success of this book. You shepherded the shepherd through this project. My name is on the front, but yours should be.

To my precious daughters, April and Autumn, you've always been special. Different yet similar. Both full of faith and fun. Both gifted and guided by God. Both beautiful and baptized, caring and responsible. You have made your mom and dad so happy and thankful. It's true what you sing with your mother, "How could we ask for more?" Your love, laughter, and life light up my world. Thank you for growing up to be virtuous women. I am always proud of you.

To Edgewood Congregational Methodist Church for taking in a young 23-year-old preacher (38 years ago) and giving him a place to serve and showing him plenty of grace many, many times through the years. Thank you. I love each and every one of you.

To the Edgewood staff—Barry, Susan, Patty, Myra, Brandon and Chris. You are the best! It's a joy to serve alongside you. You are not only fellow laborers; you are friends. I enjoy doing life with you.

To my mom, Barbara Bedgood—Your sweet faith blesses me. You've always been a great mom—Always! Thanks for a great childhood, great memories, and for always believing in me.

To my dad, William A. Snow, Sr.—the sharpest, smartest, youngest 85-year-old man I know. I hope I have your genes. You are a living example of leadership to me. I'm proud to be your son.

To my sisters, Terri and Denice—Your love and laughter always lift me. You both radiate style and class everywhere you go. You bring out the best in everyone!

To Aaron Taylor, whose friendship and prayers through the years I greatly value. I'm eternally grateful that God sent you my way. Men like you are few and far between. Thank you for the years of prayers that you prayed for me!

Most importantly, I owe everything to my Savior and Lord Jesus Christ. As a 16-year-old at an old camp meeting in Butler, Georgia, I gave my life to Christ. I haven't looked back. He made life worth living. He is my rock, my anchor, and my fortress. So, thank you, Jesus. It is the joy and privilege of my life to serve you. I pray I make a difference in Your kingdom.

INTRODUCTION

I have Congenital Ichthyosis . . . . There—I said it. It doesn't mean anything to most of you—but to the one in 200,000 people affected and afflicted with it, it can be debilitating, humiliating, and frustrating. There are different levels and different kinds of ichthyosis. Some light—some severe. It is something you live with. You try to control and contain it. It is a rare skin disorder that hinders many who have it . . . and with God's help, I determined a long time ago that I would not let it stop me from serving and doing God's will. It has been a part of me since birth and will be with me till death, until I get a new, glorified body.

I am now 61. This book is as much for me as it is you. I have had to overcome the effects of ichthyosis. The stares, the questions, the redness, the dryness, the flakes . . . but, with God's help, I have overcome—and of all things—I am a preacher! I believe and pray that I have lived what I have written about in this little book.

So yes, I can—and I will! I am doing what I am supposed to have done for several years. That is, pursing a dream and writing a book. This book is as much for me as it is for you! I hope you receive instruction, inspiration, and information from these words. But I am practicing what I preach and believe that I am doing something that stretches and challenges me. Also, I thank you for taking the time to read this book. I pray you find hope, help and healing in it, and that you too can say, "Yes, I can!"

In this book, you will find truths that transform you, principles that produce progress, and an attitude that will help you soar. This book is to be enjoyed and applied to your daily life. It has short chapters written to help you understand and apply its principles more easily.

Many of us are plagued with the thought, "I can't be that way, or I can't live that way, or I can't do that thing." Then God comes into our lives and reminds us, "Yes, with my help and my Spirit, you can!"

This is a journey of "I can!" Someone said, "Success comes in cans; failures come in can'ts." The devil will try to defeat you, discourage you, and depress you. People will try to scare you, silence you, and stop you. You may even have a bad habit of self-destruction, which can be the worst enemy of all. I learned a long time ago that the lower your self-image, the more likely you are to sabotage yourself or defeat yourself. Don't self-destruct! Don't do anything stupid or sinful. Many times, the "I cannot" comes from a deeper, "I am not."

The first rule of winning is don't beat yourself!

Three Simple Keys to Winning in Life

1. Think right—Philippians 4:8 says: "Finally, brethren, whatsoever things are true, whatsoever things are honest, whatsoever things are just, whatsoever things are pure, whatsoever things are lovely, whatsoever things are of good report; if there be any virtue, and if there be any praise, think on these things." You must think right!

2. Talk right—Proverbs 18:21 says: "Death and life are in the power of the tongue: and they that love it shall eat the fruit thereof." You must talk right!

3. Walk right—Luke writes in Chapter 10:19: "Behold, I give unto you power to tread on serpents and scorpions, and over all the power of the enemy: and nothing shall by any means hurt you." You must live right!

At the point of being victorious, hold on to God and stay there. Don't defeat yourself!

Grow! — Develop! — Dream! — Stretch!

Remember the dream is easy and free—to fulfill the dream will cost a lot of effort and energy.

David Livingston, that great missionary to Africa, said, "I love life, and I'll go anywhere as long as it's forward."

I love the story that goes like this:

> *One little boy was spending the day at his grandparents' house. After lunch, Granddad decided to take a nap. The little boy was bored and found some Limburger cheese in the refrigerator. He took some of that smelly cheese and snuck into Grandpa's bedroom and wiped some of that cheese on grandpa's mustache. He then ran out of the room giggling.*
>
> *Just a few seconds later, Grandpa woke up to that terrible smell. He didn't know what had been done, so when he inhaled through his nose, he said, "This room stinks!"*
>
> *He got up and went to the kitchen where Grandma was baking cookies. He took a big breath and said, "This kitchen stinks."*
>
> *So Grandpa walked outside to the sunshine and blue sky. He inhaled deeply, but all he could smell was that Limburger cheese that his grandson had wiped on his mustache, and Grandpa said, "The whole world stinks!"*

Don't you know some people with Limburger cheese attitudes? Everything stinks! Everything is always bad or wrong.

I hope this short, simple, and straightforward book will help you improve and have a great attitude.

So, choose now that with God's help you'll have the right attitude.

I will grow—not groan.

I will be better—not bitter.

I will win—not whine.

I will choose—not lose.

Someone once said, "You're not a born winner; you're not a born loser; you're a born chooser!"

We see that same great attitude in the Apostle Paul who, though in prison, would not stay down or be defeated. He used that prison as his pen, prayer, purpose, and pulpit to advance the kingdom of God.

When Paul wrote his letter to the Philippians, his environment was a prison, not a palace.

It was there that he writes a joy letter! He is encouraging them to find joy and contentment in any circumstance or situation. He mentions sixteen times to "have joy" or be grateful. By the time we get to Chapter 4, it is chock full of positive motivational thoughts for your life.

We learn and know passages by their content. Here are several:

- Psalm 23—The Shepherd's Psalm

- I Corinthians 13—The Love Chapter

- I Corinthians 15—The Chapter of Death

- Hebrews 11—The Faith Chapter

- John 17—Jesus High Priestly Prayer

- Philippians 4—The "I Can" Chapter

Maybe you're in the pit of depression or at your wit's end. Don't give up. Read on. Let's go! No more blame games or regrets. No more "if onlys!" Joy is an inside job! It's your personal responsibility. It wasn't only true with Paul in prison in 60 AD; it's true today.

So, start now! Start today! Let this book boost you and help you to choose to have an "I can" attitude.

I hope you enjoy this book and are encouraged by its words.

CHAPTER 1

I CAN LOVE

Therefore, my beloved and longed-for brethren, my joy and crown, so stand fast in the Lord, beloved.

Philippians 4:1 (NKJV)

By definition, the word *beloved* means "a much-loved person." God clearly and completely commands us to love. In John 13:34–35, Jesus says: "A new commandment I give unto you, That ye love one another; as I have loved you, that ye also love one another. By this shall all men know that ye are my disciples, if ye have love one to another."

Our Lord says, "They will know you are my disciples if you have love for each other." He did not say: They will know you're my disciples if . . .

1. You are ultra-talented or gifted.

2. You go to a big church.

3. You have a great personality.

4. You live a faithful life.

5. You serve all the time.

Those things are good. But He said, "They will know you are my disciples if you *love* one another."

Why do we complicate this command? Why do we make this so difficult? Twice Paul writes in verse one "dearly beloved." He emphasizes, "I love you!" He is reminding us to love one another. We live in a world that desperately needs love, yet genuine love is difficult to find. Real love is strong and it's healthy; it's a verb, a commitment. Someone defined love as, "a willingness to hurt." You can look at God or Jesus and see how He loves us. John 3:16 tells us, "For God so *loved* the world that He *gave* His only begotten son . . ." He was willing to hurt, suffer, and sacrifice for us.

I memorized a definition of love that says: "Love is the whole-hearted wish toward the well-being of another person, and the willingness to sacrifice or inconvenience oneself in order to secure their happiness." You'd do well to read that again very slowly. If that is love, then love is a verb—an action word. Paul says yes, you can love.

One young businessman relocated to a new, beautiful office complex. His first day, he rode the elevator to the twentieth floor, walked down the hall to his new spacious office, and sat down in his new and luxurious room. It was filled with pricey amenities: a contemporary desk, expensive pictures, plush carpet, and beautiful chairs. He sat there all morning with no phone calls, no mail, no clients, and no work. At noon he pulled his sack lunch from his briefcase and ate. He then waited all afternoon and still no clients, no calls, and no business. At 5:00 p.m., he gathered his papers and briefcase, and as he was starting to leave, he saw the elevator open. He ran back to his desk, jumped into his swivel chair, picked up the phone, and began to talk into the phone as the visitor approached his office. The young businessman spoke into the phone and said, "Yes, sir, we will be happy to place that order and ship those materials first thing tomorrow morning, and thank you for your business." In saying that, he turned in his chair, hung up the phone, turned to the man in front of his desk and said, "Yes, sir, and how can I help you?" to which the man replied, "Sir, I'm here to hook up your phone." I think, at times, we can be like that young businessman—fake. We put on our "church" faces, masks—facades, when people are looking, even longing, for real, genuine love. We should drop the façade, be honest and genuine, and sincerely show God's love to others.

In 2020-2021, we were in the midst of COVID-19, a world-wide pandemic. We all had to wear masks and practice social distancing. But I know people who were "wearing masks" long before COVID, pretending to be someone they aren't. What they need is, like Paul in Acts 9 . . . they need a "De Mask Us" experience (sorry, bad joke!) But loving others can't be fake or false. It must be true and honest, and that comes from a right relationship with God. I tell my staff, "You can't love the crowd and hate the people." No, no—you must love the people!

My first real church experience was Praise Tabernacle Congregational Methodist Church in Powder Springs, Georgia. It started in a small storefront building that we had to get to early and clean. As a sixteen-year-old boy, I met people who welcomed me, hugged me, and showed me genuine love. I don't think there were over thirty-five or forty people in that building, but it seemed like 350 to me! They showed me God's unconditional, warm and welcoming love. It helped change my life, and it launched me on my journey with Jesus.

The following Scriptures give evidence to this commandment:

Mark 12:29–31 says, [29]"And Jesus answered him, "The first of all the commandments is, Hear, O Israel; The Lord our God is one Lord: [30]And thou shalt love the Lord thy God with all

thy heart, and with all thy soul, and with thy entire mind, and
with all thy strength: this is the first commandment. ³¹And the
second is like, namely this, "Thou shalt love thy neighbor as
thyself. There is none other commandment greater than these."

Romans 13:8 says, "Owe no man anything, but to love one
another: for he that loveth another hath fulfilled the law."

I Corinthians 13:13 directs, "And now abideth faith, hope,
charity (love), these three; but the greatest of these is charity (love)."

I John 2:10 tells us, "He that loveth his brother abideth in the
light, and there is no occasion of stumbling in him."

I John 3:14–16 says, ¹⁴"We know that we have passed from
death unto life because we love the brethren. He that loveth
not his brother abideth in death. ¹⁵Whosoever hateth his
brother is a murderer: and ye know that no murderer hath
eternal life abiding in him. ¹⁶Hereby perceive we the love of
God because he laid down his life for us: and we ought to lay
down our lives for the brethren."

I John 4:7–11, 16, 19 instructs, ⁷"Beloved, let us love one
another: for love is of God; and everyone that loveth is born
of God and knoweth God. ⁸He that loveth not knoweth not
God; for God is love. ⁹In this was manifested the love of God
toward us because that God sent his only begotten Son into
the world, that we might live through him. ¹⁰Herein is love,
not that we loved God, but that he loved us, and sent his Son
to be the propitiation for our sins. ¹¹Beloved, if God so loved

us, we ought also to love one another. [16]And we have known and believed the love that God hath for us, God is love; and he that dwelled in love, dwelleth in God and God in him. [19]We love him, because he first loved us."

John knew about love. He wrote of himself that he "was the apostle whom Jesus loved."

Let me make this a little clearer: There is "human" love and there is "divine" love.

Human love says . . .

- "I will love you—*if* you love me."

- "I will speak to you—*if* you speak to me."

- "I will be nice to you—*if* you are nice to me."

- "I will forgive you—*if* you forgive me."

Human love is conditional—based upon the condition that you do what I want you to do!

Divine love says . . .

- "I will love you—*even if* you don't love me."

- "I will speak to you—*even if* you don't speak to me."

- "I will be nice to you—*even if* you are not nice to me."

- "I will forgive you—*even if* you don't forgive me."

Divine love is unconditional. It is not based upon others' actions, but rather on the depth of your spiritual life.

Therefore, we learn: "Yes, I can love!" With God's help, His Holy Spirit power, we can love! Divine love turns a cheek, goes a second mile, gives a shirt away, and prays for its enemies.

Jesus identified divine love this way:

Matthew 5:38–44 says: "[38]Ye have heard that it hath been said, 'An eye for an eye, and a tooth for a tooth:' [39]But I say unto you, That ye resist not evil: but whosoever shall smite thee on thy right cheek, turn to him the other also. [40]And if any man will sue thee at the law, and take away thy coat, let him have thy cloak also. [41]And whosoever shall compel thee to go a mile, go with him twain. [42]Give to him that asketh thee, and from him that would borrow of thee, turn not thou away. [43]Ye have heard that it hath been said, 'Thou shalt love thy neighbour, and hate thine enemy. [44]But I say unto you, 'Love your enemies, bless them that curse you, do good to them that hate you, and pray for them which despitefully use you, and persecute you.'"

Therefore, we learn: "Yes, I can!" (With the power and presence of the Holy Spirit.) Love!

Think about someone who needs divine love; someone who needs to experience God's wonderful love. Now—Go show them God's wonderful love!

Philippians 4:1 states, "I can love . . . with God's help."

Yes, you can love!

CHAPTER 2

I CAN BE A PEACEMAKER

I implore Euodia and I implore Syntyche to be of the same mind in the Lord.

Philippians 4:2 (NKJV)

Jesus said in Matthew 5:9, "Blessed are the peacemakers for they shall be called the children of God."

The truth is, at times, there is conflict in the church, and when reading in the New Testament book of Acts, the Epistles, and II John, you read about conflict in the church. We are not immune. As a new and young Christian, I held all believers to a higher standard and didn't know there were disagreements, arguments, and/or conflicts. I never saw it in the church where I was saved. The church was loving, kind, and filled with joy; but I never worked behind the scenes, either.

My first pastorate was part-time in a little church of eight elderly people in Mississippi. I was at Bible college, and only twenty-one years old. They met only two Sundays a month. After six months, I asked the church to meet every Sunday. They quickly voted me down, and I eventually left the church to pastor a larger, more modern church in Vicksburg, Mississippi. During the transition time, I was called into the office of the Dean of Students at Wesley College, and he asked me what I said to the people there to make them so upset. They had said I pointed my finger in their faces and told them that they needed to go door to door witnessing, and that I was rude to them. I didn't remember it like that. He told me they financially supported the college, and we might lose their support. Either way, it was an eye-opening and heart-wrenching experience of conflict for me.

At my second pastorate, I saw and heard things in the committee meetings and between people that I had never seen or heard before. Don't get me wrong; they were very good people, many Godly, but a few were . . . less than kind.

So I have learned:

1. There is conflict in the church.

2. Some people carry conflict with them.

3. When a conflict occurs, there is a right way to handle the conflict.

Here are a few conflict considerations:

God's Word gives us clear direction on handling conflict.

Matthew 18:15–17 says: "[15]Moreover, if thy brother shall trespass against thee, go and tell him his fault between thee and him alone: if he shall hear thee, thou hast gained thy brother." Matthew 18:15 KJV (one on one).

[16]But if he will not hear thee, then take with thee one or two more, that in the mouth of two or three witnesses every word may be established." Matthew 18:16 KJV (one and take someone).

[17]And if he shall neglect to hear them, tell it unto the church: but if he neglects to hear the church, let him be unto thee as an heathen man and a publican. Matthew 18:17 KJV (one with the church).

1. During conflict, always confront to heal, never to hurt. The goal is always reconciliation and redemption.

2. The right attitude in conflict and confrontation is always to show God's grace and humility, never to fight or show force. It is always more encouraging when people confront you with kindness and grace. Share the conflict with comfort. Cover the conflict with a compliment, if possible. Start by saying something nice or positive, then share the conflict, then nice again. Therefore, hopefully, minimizing the hurt.

In our scripture verse, Paul mentions two ladies in the church at Philippi who were not getting along. Their names were Euodias and Syntyche.

"Now I appeal to Euodia and Syntyche. Please, because you belong to the Lord, settle your disagreement" (Philippians 4:2 NLT).

In the Bible, many times names mean something or reflect something in a person's character or personality. If you were to study these names, and their root meanings, you would learn much about them.

Euodias (in Greek—*Euodia*) means fragrance.

Syntyche (in Greek—*Euvtuxn*) literally, means misfortune or ill-fortunate.

I Can Be a Peacemaker

Even the sound of their names, Euodia (odorous) and Syntyche (touchy), tells you there is a problem. These two ladies evidently hit heads with each other.

One goes around causing a "stink" or "odor" everywhere she goes.

The other is "super sensitive" or "touchy" about every issue. Do you know any people like that? These women had caused division and disagreement in the church, so Paul writes, "Be of the same mind; be harmonious, get along!" (Philippians 4:2).

In the church, people sing in harmony. They sing different parts, and it sounds great.

The parts complement each other. That is what we are to do in the church. Different personalities add value and insight to issues. Listen, learn, and respect other's opinions. Don't allow the devil to destroy relationships because of your personality. Someone once said, "The devil is excited when the church is divided."

From these ladies we learn the following:

1. Don't cause a stink everywhere you go!

2. Don't be super sensitive about what others say or do!

3. Even friends can have differences of opinion.

Someone said, "Everyone in the church carries two imaginary buckets. In one bucket, there is gasoline, and in the other, water." When a spark of contention rises up in the church, you have a choice. You can throw water on that spark and put it out, or you can throw gas on it and cause it to blaze, burn, and hurt a lot of people. The answer is always put water on the fire!

The big need in the church is for peacemakers.

Paul says, "I can, with God's help, be a peacemaker."

God's desire for us and the church is to have holy, healthy, and happy relationships with each other.

God has called *all* of us to be peacemakers. So today, go and "make" peace with others! You can make it happen with God's help'!

Philippians 4:2 "I can be a peacemaker . . . with God's help!"

Yes, you can be a peacemaker!

CHAPTER 3

I CAN HELP

And I urge you also, true companion, help these women who labored with me in the gospel, with Clement also, and the rest of my fellow workers, whose names are in the Book of Life.

Philippians 4:3 (NKJV)

> *"And I ask you, my true partner, to help these two*
> *women, for they worked hard with me in telling others*
> *the Good News. They worked along with Clement and*
> *the rest of my coworkers, whose names are written in the*
> *Book of Life." (Philippians 4:3 NLT)*

Paul urges true yokefellows (companions, partners, coworkers) to help those women, perhaps Euodias and Syntyche, or other Christians in the church at Phillipi who helped him in the work of the Lord. One translation says, "my true companions"; another says, "my true partners." Paul is grateful for their help. He needs their help! He is teaching us, "I can help." I love this thought.

Where I pastor, we have committee meetings. My hope is as we gather twelve people around a table or in a room that every member of that committee will bring something to the table or add something of a different perspective or experience to the issue being discussed so that the best decision can be made.

Someone joked about a committee (sarcastically), and said:

> *"There was in the beginning, a committee—and the*
> *committee was good—and the committee was fruitful*
> *and multiplied into many committees. Subcommittees*
> *were formed—and they met, and then met again with*
> *the committee to tell them what they met about—what*
> *they did—what they are doing now—and what they are*
> *going to do. In their next committee meeting, they will*
> *decide when to meet and then decide what to do about*
> *what they met about, or decide not to do what they*

*decided to do, and if they do what they decided to do,
they will meet again to decide whether it was right and
good to do so; now that is what a committee does!"*

Ahhh!

In the church, everyone has different abilities, gifts, talents, and perspectives. They should use them to benefit and bless the Kingdom of God. They should help!

We are called to help,
not hurt the situation.

We are called to help,
not hinder the situation.

We are called to help,
not harm the situation.

We are called to help,
not hate the situation.

The question is: How can *you* help?

Remember the parable in Matthew 25:14–30 where the master gave a servant five talents, another two talents, and another one talent. The servants with five and two talents used their talents for the master, and their master doubled them. The one with the one talent went and hid his, and the master strongly condemned him.

When I was at Wesley College, I attended school with a lot of five-talented people—young preachers who could sing, preach, teach, play the piano or guitar, administrate, lead, promote, and work well with people. But today, many of them are not in the ministry, or they are doing very little for the Kingdom of God. Also, I attended college with some who were not ultra-gifted or ultra-talented. They were two-talented people who now have rolled up their sleeves and gone to work for Jesus! No one can do everything! You don't have to; it's not expected, but everyone can do something. You must find your talent and be diligent and faithful to do your part! Someone once said: "I can do what you can't do, and you can do what I can't do, and together we can do great things for God!"

You can help! How? What's the key?

Obey in all things, even the small things. Live a life of complete obedience to the Lord. If we are faithful in the small things, God will trust us with other things! Maybe even greater things!

I'm saying, "Don't just sit there—serve…do something!" Help. Use your talents and abilities for Jesus. In Philippians 4:3, Paul says to help those in the church who are doing a good job!

So, what is your talent? Ability? Strength? What are you good at? Give it to Him, and use it for the glory of God, and He will multiply it. Proverbs 18:16 says: "A man's gift maketh room for him and bringeth him before great men."

Use your giftedness, and God will open doors for you and put you in places and with people you could never have imagined.

But we never force our way in or push our way to the top. Let God put you where you need to be!

So, use your giftedness, talent, ability for His glory. He gave you that ability, so use it for His glory.

What do you see that needs help? Let that burden begin your ministry. Let your passion—your heart—guide you. You don't have to be number one. Just try to help! Jesus had a servant's heart. He taught that leadership is servanthood.

He said in John 13:15–17 (NLT), "¹⁵I have given you an example to follow. Do as I have done to you. ¹⁶I tell you the truth; servants are not greater than their master. Nor is the messenger more important than the one who sends the message. ¹⁷Now that you know these things, God will bless you for doing them."

Servants do what? Serve! So go serve. Go help with the lights, go sweep or mop a floor, go clean a parking lot, or go help the elderly. Teach a class, lead a small group, usher, greet, pray. Find something to do for Christ, and do it with all your heart!

Again, Philippians 4:3 states, "And I entreat thee also, true yokefellow, help those women which labored with me in the gospel, with Clement also, and with other my fellow laborers, whose names are in the book of life."

Yes, you can help!

CHAPTER 4

I CAN REJOICE

Rejoice in the Lord always.
Again I will say, rejoice!

Philippians 4:4 (NKJV)

Paul writes from a Roman dungeon and says to "rejoice in the Lord." He uses the word *joy* or *rejoice* sixteen times in this short book. It is a major theme of this book and His life. I like what the Message translation says, "Celebrate God all day, every day— I mean revel in Him." The New Century Version says, "Be full of joy in the Lord always, I will say again—be full of joy."

Paul's in prison, with troubles and trials, problems and persecution, and yet he commands us and reminds us to "Rejoice in the Lord always."

There was a psychiatrist and psychologist convention, and one of the projects was to define "life." They broke off into small groups and came up with a paragraph defining life. The conference leader determined that a paragraph was too long to understand and told them to go back and define life in one sentence. After much discussion and difficulty, they came back with a one-sentence definition of life. After reviewing the sentence, the conference leader told them to go back and condense that sentence to one word in describing life. After much discussion, they came back with a one-word definition of life.

They determined, "Life is stress." Can you relate? Life's responsibilities? Relationships? Problems? Deadlines? Finances? Health? But Paul teaches us that life in Christ has an inner peace and contentment. There is purpose and a great sense of well-being. There is joy!

The verse reads: "Rejoice in the Lord always and again I say rejoice." I'll be honest with you; there is one word that gives me difficulty. Do you see it? The word *always*. It's easy to rejoice when things are going well; when the bills are paid, marriage is good, kids are happy, everyone is healthy, and church is growing, and you have spiritual victory. But can I (we) rejoice when life is not easy, when health is failing, kids are rebelling, marriage is struggling, church is frustrating, and bills are past due?

What is this verse really saying? I think I see it: "Rejoice in the Lord always and again I say rejoice." When I was in college, I quickly fell in love with a beautiful young lady named Myra. It was love at first sight. She was a blue-eyed, blonde-haired beauty (and still is!). Actually, she sang at my sister Denice's wedding, and I noticed her there. Then I saw her again at Wesley College about one year later. I began the pursuit to know her better. Then one evening as I was in the dorm room at Wesley College studying for math, I got bored—simply bored!

After ten minutes of studying, I left my dorm room and went to the administrative building to see friends and play ping-pong (I majored in ping-pong). After 30 minutes of that, I walked down the hall and passed the cafeteria where there were a lot of students studying. I looked in and saw the lady of my dreams, Myra. So I made my way over to her table and asked her, "What are you doing?"

She replied, "Studying."

I confidently asked, "Can I help?" Then for the next two hours I helped her study one of the toughest courses at Wesley

College: Systematic Theology. We had our tests the next day. I should have taken the systematic theology exam . . . I would have done better than I did on the math test. But what happened with my studying and attention? Earlier in the dorm, I did not want to study—then thirty minutes later, I spent the next two and a half hours "studying" a very difficult course.

What was the difference? Did I have some great spiritual experience between my dorm room and the cafeteria that made me want to study?

No! No! A thousand times No!

Was I filled with the power and presence of the Lord on my way to the cafeteria?

No! The difference in the dorm room and cafeteria was Myra! She was the object of my affection, the focus of my attention. My focus was on Myra, not on the studying. Now, what does that verse say?

Rejoice in your problems? Rejoice in your trials? Rejoice in your troubles? No.

It says, "Rejoice in the Lord" He is always good, and He is always wonderful! The focus of your attention and the object of your affections are always on Him—not your problems, struggles, hurts, or hang ups!

That leads me to two quick thoughts:

1. The best witness you can have is to be a joyful or rejoicing Christian! While the world walks in darkness and stress, we walk in peace and joy! One Christian said, "I wake up every morning with purpose, meaning, and direction. Let them see Christ in you!"

2. Celebrate God all day long. The Message translation says in Philippians 4:4, "Celebrate God all day, every day, I mean revel in Him." Celebrate God! We celebrate birthdays, anniversaries, births, ball team wins; we should celebrate Jesus! He is a wonderful Savior!

One sweet lady in our church (we called her the mayor of Alexandria), Mrs. Mary Jo McMichael said, "If we love the Lord, we need to let our face know it."

Let your face know it—and it all starts with focusing on Jesus!

Philippians 4:4, "Rejoice in the Lord always and again I say rejoice."

Yes, you can rejoice!

CHAPTER 5

I CAN BE DISCIPLINED (SELF-CONTROLLED)

*Let your gentleness
be known to all men.
The Lord is at hand.*

Philippians 4:5 (NKJV)

Here is Philippians 4:5 in several versions:

NASB: "Let your gentle spirit be known to all men. The Lord is near."

ASV: "Let your forbearance be known unto all men. The Lord is at hand."

ESV: "Let your reasonableness be known to everyone. The Lord is at hand."

GOOD NEWS: "Show a gentle attitude toward everyone. The Lord is coming soon."

NLT: "Let everyone see that you are considerate in all you do. Remember, the Lord is coming soon."

MESSAGE: "Make it as clear as you can to all you meet that you're on their side, working with them and not against them. Help them see that the Master is about to arrive. He could show up any minute!"

NKJ: "Let your gentleness be known to all men. The Lord is at hand."

NIV: "Let your gentleness be evident to all. The Lord is near."

This Word tells me that I can be self-controlled, kind, reasonable and gentle . . . I can have a good attitude. In the original language, some of the words read like this:

> *"Let your (Epikes) fairness, reasonableness, suitableness, or patience, be known, perceived, revealed, to all men, the Lord is (eggus) near, or there with you."*

I believe the thrust of the verse teaches us that with God's help, we are to have an attitude of being controlled, fair, balanced, or kind and that He is with you.

He is saying, "With God's help, I can be balanced, fair and self-controlled." It could be explained as, "Let your gentleness, unselfishness, kindness, be perceived by everyone, the Lord is with you."

We quickly learn:

1. This is the way believers should behave! As Christ has changed us, we care about fairness and balance. Proverbs 11:1, "The Lord loves a fair and just balance."

2. We are not to be unbalanced or unreasonable. Christians aren't "rioters," "ragers," or "rowdy:" But now you must also rid yourselves of all such things as these: anger, rage, malice, slander, and filthy language from your lips. Colossians 3:8 (NIV).

3. We don't lose our cool or our control. Do you
    know anyone around with whom you always have
    to walk on eggshells? You never know how they
    are going to respond. These Christians are bad
    witnesses to the world. They are different every
    day! One day they are up, and one day they are
    down—one day happy and one day upset. They
    are unapproachable, or supersensitive, or they
    "blow up" easily.

Years ago, I remember waiting in line for thirty minutes to get a
new driver's license and the picture. I went during lunch and was
hoping for a quick process. It did not turn out that way. I finally
got up to the desk only to see a sign that said they do not accept
debit cards. All I had was a debit card—no cash, no check. I
double checked with the cashier, and she apologized. I wanted
to say things like, "You're kidding me!" or "Ya'll need to get up
to date" or "Put a sign at the door rather than at the counter," or
some other smart remark about not taking debit cards.

I told the lady I understood and would be back later. When I
did come back, the line was shorter, and the cashier and I had
a chance to talk.

She recognized me from earlier and knew that I was the pastor
at Edgewood Church, and said she may try to join us one
Sunday for worship.

What if I had gotten upset, mad, or said some things that
could have been cutting? My witness would have been ruined,
but I remained balanced, calm, controlled.

There is an old saying: "If you treat everyone you come in contact with like they were hurting, you'd be treating 90% of the people correctly." Give people the benefit of the doubt. Give people grace and an "out." As Dale Carnegie says, "Let them save face."

Again Philippians 4:5 says, "Let your moderation be known unto all men. The Lord is at hand." It says "unto all men."

1. Not just the ones you like.

2. Not just the ones you accept.

3. Not just the ones who like you.

4. Not just the ones who look like you!

Let everyone see your balanced, controlled, and reasonable life! This is spiritual maturity. This is accepting responsibility. I have a little sign in my office at home that says, "I'll be where I'm supposed to be, when I'm supposed to be there, if not sooner." It speaks to me of a self-controlled life.

This verse in Philippians 4:5 teaches me I must lead myself first, and that's the toughest person of all to lead. Someone said, "When we try to conquer the world, we are foolish, but when we try to conquer ourselves, we are wise."

We live in a world of excess. More. Plenty.

We want happiness, and we want it now.

We want wealth, and we want it now.

We want health, and we want it now.

I would say Jesus is the first and the center of your life and your life must be balanced. Don't die before you die. John Wesley prayed, "Lord, help me never to outlive my usefulness." Johnathan Edwards had seventy resolutions to live by and one said, "I am resolved to live with all my might while I do live." Former U.S. President George W. Bush said at his dad's funeral, "Dad wanted to die young as late as possible." Isn't that true for us? Don't die before you die. Craig Groeschel, that great pastor of Life church said, "I wake up every morning with purpose, direction, and meaning."

John Wesley traveled an average of twenty miles a day on horse-back for over forty years. He got up every morning at 4:00 a.m. He preached 40,000 sermons, wrote 400 books, knew 10 languages and at the age of 83, he was annoyed that he couldn't work more than fifteen hours a day. At age 86, he was ashamed he couldn't preach more than twice a day. Perhaps this feeling is why he prayed, "Lord, help me never to outlive my usefulness."

We can and should be disciplined. It is a lifelong journey; a lifelong practice. You ask, "What if I fail?" Then try again tomorrow.

I am now 61 years old. Someone once said, "When I was a young man, I wanted to change the world." As I got older, I wanted to change my friends and family. Now I realize I need to change myself. That is the key!

This verse tells me to be consistent, not moody. To be balanced, disciplined, self-controlled, and have a good attitude . . . even when I don't feel like it.

Philippians 4:5, commands, "Let your moderation be known unto all men. The Lord is at hand."

Yes, you can
be disciplined!

CHAPTER 6

I CAN PRAY

*Be anxious for nothing,
but in everything by prayer
and supplication, with
thanksgiving, let your
requests be made known
to God;*

Philippians 4:6 (NKJV)

This is a great passage that builds on each statement.

The first lesson from this verse is "not to worry." If you are a worrier, these verses are for you!

Vance Havner, a great country preacher (1901–1986) said, "Worry is a lot like a rocking chair; it will give you something do to, but it won't get you anywhere." This verse is a prescription on how to defeat worry and anxiety. God does not want us to be worriers. Instead, we can have wonderful peace. (That's found in verse 7).

The second lesson is that instead of worrying, we should pray. There are three types or levels of prayer in this verse.

Prayer is . . . asking or talking to God.

Supplication is . . . humbly bringing your needs before the Lord; bowing before Him and giving Him your needs. Acknowledging that you cannot do anything or fix it by yourself.

Thanksgiving is . . . being and saying "thank you" to God for all you are going through; whether it is a problem, trial, heartache, or a blessing, gift, or victory.

People think and say, "I can't pray."

I want to stop them and say, "Yes, you can!" This is the one ministry we can all do!

I Can Pray

You say, "I'm not a pretty pray*er* or I get my words mixed up."

That's ok! I'm not a pretty pray*er*, either.

I know some pretty pray*ers*. When they pray, they say pretty words, and it flows from their heart, and they seem to melt and humble themselves and be in touch with God. It is a beautiful thing. My wife, Myra, prays that way. A great friend of ours, Shelia Martin, is also a "pretty pray*er*." When they pray, the atmosphere changes; it's a wonderful and amazing thing. I believe they have the gift of intercession.

Let me break prayer into three areas for you. When you pray you probably fall into one of these three groups.

1. Worship—You bow before Him, you break, and you humble yourself and honor God. When you pray, you worship. Your voice may change; your attitude may change, for you are in the presence of a Holy God.

2. Warfare—When you pray, you are ready for battle. You want to charge the gates of hell. You want to defeat the enemy now. You pray with force and with faith. You declare victory and defeat over the devil. Prayer is a means of advancement for you.

3. Work—For many, prayer is work. It doesn't come naturally. You know you are to pray and spend time with God, yet prayer is difficult for you. The words don't flow, and you pray because you love

37

God and it is the right thing to do. Sometimes you
pray without feelings, and sometimes you pray
having to exercise your faith.

I believe the greatest thing I have done for my spiritual life
and ministry is to become a person of prayer. When I began
my ministry, I quickly realized the fruit and result of ministry
came from my closeness to God. Prayer was the key. I was not
a "pretty pray*er*," but I knew the importance of prayer. So, I
became committed to spending much time with God in prayer.

There are those who "don't pray" or say they "can't pray." They
are afraid of saying the "wrong" thing or embarrassing themselves. That shouldn't stop you.

Many years ago, at Indian Springs campground, three of the
preachers were Dr. Paul Rees, Dr. Jimmy Lentz, and Dr. John
Maxwell. I played golf one afternoon and caught up with
them. I played several holes with them. After I got to know
them better, they invited me to pray the next day at the camp
meeting before Dr. Maxwell preached. What a great privilege
and opportunity!

I began to pray about my prayer. That afternoon came, and
I got up there to pray. My mind went blank. I stumbled in
prayer by saying, "Lord, thank you for this day, for Brother
John Maxwell . . . and, uh, for this camp . . . in your wonderful
name, Amen." That was pretty close to being it.

I was embarrassed and ashamed. I walked past those spiritual
giants humiliated and defeated.

They shook my hand and said, "Thank you."

I sat in that congregation, and the devil jumped all over me, saying, "That was a pitiful prayer. You are a pitiful pray*er*. You shouldn't pray!"

I had to rebuke the devil and recommit myself to being a person of prayer!

Not long after that, a community near my home called Choccolocco had their 150th anniversary with an arts and craft day. I was invited as the Pastor of Edgewood Congregational Methodist Church to come at 7 a.m. and open with prayer. I didn't think much of it until I arrived and was seated on a platform with state and local officials. This "little" event suddenly became an "important" event. They quickly welcomed everyone and introduced me. As I stepped up to the podium, I thought, "How do I pray for Choccolocco Day?" I wondered—Do I pray for the arts and crafts—What do I do? So I prayed, "Lord, thank you for this day; thank you for this community; bless us with . . . a good day . . . Amen." I turned around to go back to my chair and thought, "What a pitifully weak prayer!

And the devil said, "You're a terrible pray*er*; quit praying!"

Well, to say the least, I had to rebuke the devil and do some spiritual warfare again!

Many years ago, Myra and I were coming back home to Alabama from visiting with family in Georgia. When we got home about 2 a.m., the girls were asleep in the back of the van. (That was before the days of car seats).

We picked them up and tucked them in. Myra and I got in bed and were exhausted. We've always prayed together before going to sleep. Since Myra is a better, longer, prettier prayer than I, I quickly said, "I'll pray." I began praying by thanking the Lord for traveling mercies, the kids, and our family . . . then my mind slowly drifted away and to sleep. I proceeded to pray for the food, that God would bless it to our bodies . . . at that moment Myra laughed. That woke me up and I quickly changed my prayer to, "Bless the spiritual food that we receive daily from your hands." Myra didn't buy it. She broke out in laughter, and so did I. I messed up in prayer.

My lesson—should I quit praying? No, a thousand times—No! Neither should you. If you mess up in prayer or feel awkward praying (and you will!), or if you don't pray "pretty" prayers, keep on praying. God knows your heart! Prayer is essential. Prayer is key. You can pray!

Max Lucado says, "When we work—we work, but when we pray—God works."

Rev. E. M. Bounds said, "Prayer doesn't prepare us for our greatest work—prayer is the greatest work." Prayer is our highest calling.

Prayer is the need of the hour.

Philippians 4:6 says, "Be careful for nothing; but in everything by prayer and supplication with thanksgiving let your requests be made known unto God."

Yes, you can pray!

CHAPTER 7

I CAN HAVE PEACE

and the peace of God, which surpasses all understanding, will guard your hearts and minds through Christ Jesus.

Philippians 4:7 (NKJV)

Peace is hard to define, but you know when you don't have it. Someone once said, "Peace is the absence of war." For Christians, it can be the absence of war with God and with people. I believe only God can give real peace. It comes in a right relationship with God through Jesus Christ.

Great Bible verses on peace read like this:

- Psalm 29:11—"The Lord will give strength unto his people; the Lord will bless his people with peace."

- Isaiah 26:3—"Thou wilt keep him in perfect peace whose mind is stayed on thee."

- Isaiah 48:22—"There is no peace, saith the Lord, unto the wicked."

- John 14:27—"Peace I leave with you, my Peace I give unto you not as the world giveth give I unto you. Let not your heart be troubled, neither let it be afraid."

- II Corinthians 13:11—"Finally, Brethren, farewell. Be perfect, be of good comfort, be of one mind, live in peace; and the God of love and peace shall be with you."

- Galatians 4:22—"But the fruit of the Spirit is love, joy, peace, long-suffering, gentleness, goodness, kindness, faith."

- Ephesians 2:14—"For He is our peace, who hath made both one, and hath broken down the middle wall of partition between us."

- Colossians 3:15—"And let the peace of God rule in your hearts, to the which also ye are called in one body: and be ye thankful."

- II Thessalonians 3:16—"Now the Lord of peace himself give you peace always by all means. The Lord be with you all."

- II Timothy 2:22—"Flee also youthful lusts: but follow righteousness, faith, charity, peace, with them that call on the Lord out of a pure heart."

He provides us a life of peace for our hearts and minds.

I believe most of us live far below the promises, privileges, and peace that God gives us. Peace—even in the midst of storms and stress, trials and tribulation, God gives peace!

Let's walk through this verse: Philippians 4:7 . . . "And the peace of God which passes all understanding, shall 'keep'— 'guard'— (it's a military word—to guard you, protect you, like a strong castle that can't be overtaken); your heart (affections and passions) and mind (judgment and understanding) through Christ Jesus."

Peace is not the absence of conflict, but it is the presence of Jesus. It is your complete trust in Jesus. It is handling conflict, problems, and issues correctly because of our relationship with Him. It is seeing that God is bigger than any Goliath or giant (problem) that we have. It is a well-being because of a right relationship with God and with others. We don't worry—instead, we have peace.

Give your all to God today and ask Him to give you His peace! Give your heart and hurts to God.

Give your triumphs and trials to God. Give your success and sorrow to God. Give your happiness and hang-ups to God. Give your burdens and blessings to God.

I have known many sad stories of Christians who have endured great heartache and suffered the sorrow of losing a loved one. Some saints in the church I pastor have lost children, and some have lost all of their children. A lovely lady in my congregation who lost all of her children still fights the fight of faith with peace. She sits in the congregation with a calmness and strength about her that only God can give.

The story that comes to my heart is about a song that my wife, Myra, sings. It's a classic, Horatio A. Spafford's famous hymn, "It is Well with My Soul." One Sunday, years ago as my wife prepared to sing that song, I got up to introduce the song before she sang. I told the congregation this story.

Horatio was a prominent lawyer of a large law firm in Chicago. In the spring of 1871, Horatio invested a large amount of money in real estate north of Chicago. In October of 1871, the Great Chicago fire reduced Chicago to ashes. He lost his large investment. That year, his four-year-old son died of scarlet fever. Two years later, in 1873, Horatio's wife, Anna, and their four daughters were crossing the Atlantic. He had to stay behind because of business and was to catch up a few days later. His family planned to vacation in England and visit his good friend, Reverend D. L. Moody. The ship was called the Ville du Havre. On November 22, 1873, while crossing the Atlantic, somehow that night the sterling ship was hit by an iron sailing vessel, killing 226 people, including all of Horatio and Anna's daughters. His wife, Anna, survived this terrible tragedy and nightmare. Upon arriving in England, she sent a telegram back to Horatio which read, "Saved alone." As Horatio sailed to his wife days later, the captain showed Horatio the place of the wreck and loss of his daughters. It is at that place that he began to write the powerful hymn, "It Is Well with My Soul."

The first verse reads like this:

> *"When peace like a river attendeth my way, When sorrows like sea billows roll; Whatever my lot, Thou hast taught me to say, It is well; it is well with my soul."*

Peace—only God can give peace in the midst of tragic loss. Later, Horatio and Anna moved from Chicago to Israel to begin working with the poor and indigent. Only God can change a life and give peace like that!

Paul realizes that the heart and the mind are the battlefields that Satan will attack. He says, "Put up a military guard. Keep an invasion from taking place in your heart and mind. Protect your heart and mind! Paul tells us how to do that in the next two verses. So keep reading—explore them with me, and live in the powerful peace that Jesus gives. I tell you from personal experience—you'll be glad you did.

Philippians 4:7 says, "And the peace of God which passeth all understanding shall keep your heart and minds through Christ Jesus."

Yes, you can have peace!

CHAPTER 8

I CAN THINK RIGHT

Finally, brethren, whatever things are true, whatever things are noble, whatever things are just, whatever things are pure, whatever things are lovely, whatever things are of good report, if there is any virtue and if there is anything praiseworthy-- meditate on these things.

Philippians 4:8 (NKJV)

I wish we all thought correctly—That is, that we all thought Biblically! Reasons we don't think correctly:

1. Bad past experiences with hurts and heartaches. (This is key.)

2. We don't realize the importance (short-term & long-term) of thinking right.

3. It's all we've ever seen or heard others do. (Those around us think wrong.)

4. We don't understand that it is a choice.

Did you hear about the guy who had to quit going to football games? Every time the team got in the huddle, he thought they were talking about him! Zig Ziglar, that great motivator said, "Most people suffer from "stinkin' thinkin'."

In counseling, three out of four people are thinking wrong about their problem.

Dr. John Maxwell taught years ago, "Your problem is not your problem; how you handle the problem is the problem."

Most people don't think "possibility thinking" or "win-win" for problem solving; they think small, narrow, and in a box. We must think right!

I served as chairman of the Alabama Camp board for many years. Alabama Camp is an old-fashioned camp that meets once a year at a small country community called Pleasant Gap, Alabama. One year while I was serving as chairman, a young man whom I'll call John came up to me and told me he had drawn pictures of Satan, demons, and hell, and excitedly asked if I would like to see them."

I quickly said, "No!" I told him he was spending his time thinking about demons and hell and all the wrong things. He needed to think about God, Jesus, the Holy Spirit, Heaven, angels—not demonic things.

Your thinking will lead to your living. Wrong thinking will lead to wrong living or bad choices, and right thinking will lead to good living and better choices.

This passage tells us to think on these things:

1. True—Not only accurate and factual things, but for believers, those things aligned with the Word of God. It tells me not to be imagining or inventing in my mind false or fearful things that may not be accurate.

2. Honest—honorable, noble

3. Just—right, correct, righteous

4. Pure—not corrupt, acceptable to God

5. Lovely—good, nice, loveable

6. Good report—admirable, winsome, gracious

If there is any virtue (superior character, moral excellence, beyond reproach); if there is any praise (anything with praise or excellence); think (fix your mind—meditate) on these things. This is the meaning of the passage found in Philippians 4:8.

What you allow to occupy your mind, sooner or later, determines your speech and actions.

The devil or demons can throw things into your mind.

You choose what you keep and think about. We cast out evil or impure thoughts, and we dwell on good and Biblical thoughts. We must allow the right things to occupy our minds. These verses are pro-active and intentional. Put the right things in your mind. Read the right books. Listen to the right podcasts. Watch the right shows and movies. Have positive friends.

Think optimistically. The Bible says in Proverbs 23:7, "As a man thinketh in his heart, so is he."

To quote an ancient Chinese proverb, "You can't keep a bird from flying over your head, but you can keep him from making a nest in your hair." You may not be able to keep a wrong thought from entering your mind, but you can keep it from staying there.

I love the story about Charlie Brown and Lucy. They were on a cruise (true story . . . LOL) going up to the deck to "catch some rays; to lie out in the sunshine."

Lucy, the psychiatrist of the group, (She could solve any problem for a nickel) immediately saw a lesson. She said, "Charlie Brown, do you see those people at the front of the ship? They set their deck chairs toward the front of the ship. They are looking forward to life, looking ahead. They are positive people. And, Charlie Brown, do you see those people at the back of the boat? They've set their deck chairs toward the back. They are the ones looking back on life, looking at where they have been, remembering the past. Now, Charlie Brown, where are you gonna put your deck chair?"

To this, Charlie Brown, with a terrible look on his face and the deck chair wrapped around his neck like a noose, replied, "I don't know! I can't even get my deck chair open!" Haven't you been there?

1. We've been there in our spiritual lives.

2. We've been there in our marriages.

3. We've been there in our parenting.

4. We've been there in our health.

5. We've been there is our finances.

6. We've been there in our relationships.

We didn't know if we were going forward or backward. We couldn't even get our deck chair open. My point is: Where will you put your deck chair?

It is your choice. This verse—like all the other verses, gives us a choice. This may be one of the toughest ones. Verse 8 tells us that "I can think right, or I can choose to think wrong. It is my choice!"

Philippians 4:8 directs, "Finally, Brethren, whatsoever things are true, whatsoever things are honest, whatsoever things are just, whatsoever things are lovely, and whatsoever things are of good report: if there be any virtue, if there be any praise, think on these things."

Yes, you can think right!

CHAPTER 9

I CAN DO RIGHT

The things which you learned and received and heard and saw in me, these do, and the God of peace will be with you.

Philippians 4:9 (NKJV)

I can do right!

Paul wouldn't tell us to do right if we couldn't do right! Biblically, we do not have to go around and live a dismal or defeated life. We can live right.

We (with Christ's power) can behave properly and live obediently, triumphantly, and victoriously. Paul, in Romans 8:37, tells us that "We are more than conquerors through Him who loves us."

Seven times in the Scripture, Paul said, "Follow me because I follow Christ." Paul knew the power of a Godly example and influence. The questions become:

1. Who are the people you lead or whom do you influence?

2. Who are the people you follow or that influence you?

John Maxwell has said the greatest motivation principle he knows is "People do what people see." We imitate others. We learn by watching others. Someone once said, "Your actions speak so loud, I can't hear a word you say."

We learned in childhood, "Imitation is the highest form of flattery." So go—set an example! Do right! Be a leader! Set the bar high for yourself, and watch others watch and follow you.

I have had the privilege to preach several camp meetings. I watched at one camp meeting as two teenagers watched my every move. I quickly realized that they probably wouldn't remember what I was going to say, but they would remember how I behaved. People watch your life, so do right!

Notice also the verse says, "If you do right, the God of peace will be with you." Here are three thoughts on peace:

1. I got "peace with God" when I got saved. I surrendered and stopped fighting or warring with God. In my surrender to God, I found peace with God.

2. I got "the peace of God" when I fully surrendered and yielded my will to His will for my life. He flooded my life with His presence, peace and purpose.

3. We are promised peace with God if we follow His plan. Do you see the five steps to peace in these verses?

   A. First, pray—[6]Be careful for nothing; (Don't worry about anything!) but in everything by prayer and supplication with thanksgiving, let your requests be made known unto God.

   Prayer is simply talking to God. Taking your needs to God; spending time with Him and in His presence.

B. Then, you supplicate—[6]Be careful for nothing; but in everything by prayer and supplication with thanksgiving, let your requests be made known unto God.

I have learned that supplication is the surrendering of my need to God. It is humbling myself and giving the situation to God.

C. Then, be thankful—[6]Be careful for nothing; but in everything by prayer and supplication with thanksgiving, let your requests be made known unto God.

You say, "Thank you," for that situation (and mean it)! This may take time, but it is essential. Then you get the peace of God. Philippians 4:7 says, "And the peace of God, which passeth all understanding, shall keep your hearts and minds through Christ Jesus."

Then, when you get peace, continue:

D. Think right—[8]Finally, brethren, whatsoever things are true, whatsoever things are honest, whatsoever things are just, whatsoever things are pure, whatsoever things are lovely, whatsoever things are of good report; if there be any virtue, and if there be any praise, think on these things.

E. Finally—Do right—[9]Those things, which ye
have both learned, and received, and heard,
and seen in me, do: and the God of peace
shall be with you.

After this process, we do right! The result is having the wonderful "peace of God" in our lives. Peace, it seems to be so
absent in people's lives, and even in believers' lives, but it
shouldn't be absent! Years ago in my life, I made a simple, and
yet powerful commitment to the Lord. When God speaks, I
simply say, "Yes, Lord!"

Do you remember when Simon Peter said no to Jesus? In John
13, Jesus was in the upper room with His disciples, teaching
and sharing the Passover meal. Jesus picked up a towel and
a basin of water and began to wash the disciples' feet. When
Jesus got to Simon Peter, Simon said, "No, Lord, you shall
never wash my feet." Jesus continued His lesson, (John 13:8),
"If I don't wash your feet, you have no part with me."

Wow! Did you catch the importance of that? You have no part
with me!!!

Simon certainly wanted to be a part of Jesus' team, so he stuck
out his feet, his hands, and his head and said, "Lord, then
wash all of me."

My point is, you can't say, "No, Lord." The minute you say no,
He ceases to be Lord. It is always, "Yes, Lord." To have peace
with God, it is always "Yes, Lord."

Please realize that partial obedience is not obedience. Selective obedience is not obedience. Our walk with God is one of complete surrender and obedience.

Isaiah 48:22 warns, "There is no peace, saith the Lord, to the wicked." You can't have a wrong relationship with Jesus and have peace with God. No way! Only Jesus gives real, lasting, genuine peace. The world offers false hope and false peace; but Jesus offers sweet and satisfying peace.

John 14:27 tells us: "Peace I leave with you, my peace I give unto you: not as the world giveth, give I unto you. Let not your heart be troubled, neither let it be afraid."

The issue is that peace comes with obedience and surrender. Follow Christ fully and He gives an inner joy and peace, but it comes through obeying the Lord.

Philippians 4:9 says, "Those things which you learned and received and heard and seen in me, do, and the God of peace will be with you."

Yes, you can do right!

CHAPTER 10

I CAN BE THANKFUL

But I rejoiced in the Lord greatly that now at last your care for me has flourished again; though you surely did care, but you lacked opportunity.

Philippians 4:10 (NKJV)

Philippians 4:10 NLT says, "How I praise the Lord that you are concerned about me again. I know you have always been concerned for me, but you didn't have the chance to help me."

Philippians 4:10 The Message states, "I'm glad in God, far happier than you would ever guess—happy that you're again showing such strong concern for me. Not that you ever quit praying and thinking about me. You just had no chance to show it."

It evidently had been a while since the Philippians had helped Paul. But now they are supporting and giving to him again. Paul never made financial demands of his converts. He never went out and gathered up financial support for himself. He does strongly teach and encourage believers to give to the Lord in I Corinthians. But here he is thanking believers for their gracious and generous gift to him.

Paul was originally a tent maker. He was self-supporting. His priority was never money—but souls! His heart's desire was to promote the message of salvation to all people.

He teaches us the proper response to gifts is to receive them with grace and thankfulness. We should look people in the eye and say, "Thank you." Don't mumble. Don't walk away. Look at them and say, "Thank you." The word *thanksgiving* is mentioned over 140 times in the Bible. I believe it grieves the Lord for His people to have a murmuring, complaining, and ungrateful spirit. Paul tells Timothy in II Timothy 3:2 that in the last days, people will become "unthankful." Certainly, we are living in those days. It pleases God for us to be grateful, thankful, and have a praising spirit.

I Can Be Thankful

Here is the key about verse 10 and giving thanks. Thanks are to be "given," not merely said. Do you see that? Saying thanks is good manners, and we should do that. Truly giving thanks is an act of worship:

- Leviticus 22:29—"And when ye will offer a sacrifice of thanksgiving unto the Lord, offer it at your own will."

- Psalm 50:14—"Offer unto God thanksgiving; and pay thy vows unto the most High."

- Psalm 100:4—"Enter into his gates with thanksgiving, and into his courts with praise: be thankful unto him, and bless his name."

- Psalm 116:17—"I will offer to thee the sacrifice of thanksgiving, and will call upon the name of the Lord."

- Col. 3:15—"And let the peace of God rule in your hearts, to which also you were called in one body, and be thankful."

A thankful spirit and/or attitude is something you give, offer, or practice because you are truly grateful and realize it's who you are in Christ.

We don't offer thanks merely to offer thanks out of ritual or without meaning or heart. That is empty. In Christ we realize everything we are and have is a gift from God. It's all His. The

Psalmist in Psalm 24:1 says, "The earth is the Lord's and the fullness thereof; the world, and they that dwell therein." We are stewards. We are managers of everything God has given us, and we are very grateful for everything He has done for us and everything He has given us.

I remember when our two girls were little. One Christmas morning we opened all the big gifts first then moved on to the stockings. The stockings were small, seemingly insignificant gifts; mostly candy, pencils, stickers, and gum. I quickly realized and saw the look on their faces that they were as happy, even thrilled with the small gifts that seemed insignificant as they were with the more expensive, larger gifts. These gifts were appreciated, and I was so very grateful that they had learned the great value of thankfulness.

One of the best men I have ever known was Roy Ledbetter, a great deacon, head usher, and a loving leader. I pastored Roy for almost thirty years. If I heard him once—I've heard him a thousand times pray and thank the Lord for shoes on his feet, the shirt on his back, the roof over his head, and food on his table. He showed, led, practiced, taught, and often reminded me to be thankful for every blessing of life.

Our church—Edgewood Church—built the first permanent building on the Buvuma Island, in Uganda, Africa, in 1998. It is used as a church, a school, a medical clinic, and a leadership training center. While visiting on the island, I had no ice, no running water, no restroom (a hole in the ground behind a wall of trees), no modern comforts, and no extra clothes— they got lost by the airline. By the time I got back home, I was so very thankful for everything God had blessed me with. I realized that I had so much and understood why people kissed the ground when they got off the plane!

I am reminded in Acts 16 of Paul and Silas. They were beaten, bloody, and bruised, but at midnight they prayed and sang praises to God and the prisoners heard them.

So, thankfulness is a scriptural and spiritual issue. You can be thankful! You should be thankful. You can change that critical or lethargic attitude to a grateful attitude. You can become that person. The Power of Christ can transform you.

Philippians 4:10 says, "But I rejoiced in the Lord greatly, that now at the last your care of me hath flourished: wherein ye were also careful, but ye lacked opportunity."

Yes, you can be thankful!

CHAPTER 11

I CAN BE CONTENT

Not that I speak in regard to need, for I have learned in whatever state I am, to be content:

Philippians 4:11 (NKJV)

Contentment is defined as "A state of mind in which one's desires are confined to his lot whatever it may be." Contentment is the opposite of envy, avarice, and anxiety. Contentment comes from humility. Materialism seems to be America's god. Contentment is not a virtue of our day. As a matter of fact, what we see in most people, even Christians, is an attitude of discontentment. We want what we want, and we want it now, and we want it our way! We want our style, our preferences, our color, our brand, our model. Things become obsolete in six months, and we want to upgrade and to have the newer model.

Today, it's not just having things; it's having the right thing, the popular thing, and the newest thing. People believe the key to happiness and fulfillment in life is having things. It's not! I taught my girls, "Things are just things." That's all they are. Things are not wrong, and a lot of times do make life better; but as an end in themselves, they are empty!

I have two simple rules for "things:"

1. God always comes first. "But seek ye first the kingdom of God, and his righteousness; and all these "things" shall be added unto you" (Matt. 6:33).

2. We are stewards, not owners, of what we have. "The earth is the Lord's, and the fullness thereof; the WORLD, and they that dwell therein" (Psalm 24:1).

Paul's view of life is that he was content in whatever circumstance or situation he found himself.

This word *content*; it's the only place this Greek word is used in the Bible. It implies that we don't let our circumstances dictate, control, or determine our attitude or behavior. He's not even implying that we control the circumstances. He is saying, as a follower of Christ, I have learned through my walk with Christ not to let circumstances control me, affect me, or "mess me up." Our lesson is: "We can't and won't always be able to control our circumstances—but we can control our response to them!" It's like the saying, "It's not what happens *to* me that is important—it's what happens *in* me." Paul lists some of the things in verse 12 that can happen to you:

Whether we are abased or abound . . . Whether we are hungry or have plenty . . . Whether we suffer or are safe . . . Whether we are humble or happy . . .

The New Century Version says in Verse 11: "I am not telling you this because I need anything. I have learned to be satisfied with the things I have and with everything that happens." This is Christian growth. This is dying to self. Notice: Paul mentions both painful and pleasant, and he's content in both. That's true contentment!

What brought Paul's contentment? He tells us in II Cor. 3:5.

- KJV: "Not that we are sufficient of ourselves to think anything as of ourselves; but our sufficiency is of God."

- NCV: "We are not saying that we can do this work ourselves. It is God who makes us able to do all that we do."

Paul realized that it was God in him. He made God the center of his life! So whatever we must go through, it must be about Him as long as Christ is glorified or seen in us.

Lessons to Learn

1. Give everything to God. Everything! The good, the bad, and the ugly.

2. Allow God to determine the value or meaning behind everything you go through.

To do this, you must:

1. Reflect on it—Pause and think about it. (Most never do this.)

2. Pray about it—Take it to the Lord in prayer.

3. Learn from it—What did God teach you through it?

4. Grow from it—What value did it add to your life?

5. Be content in it—I have peace and I thank the Lord for it.

6. Share Christ because of it—Tell others your story.

We will always have painful issues, hurts and heartaches, spills and chills, bumps and bruises.

John 16: 33 tells us: "These things I have spoken unto you, that in me ye might have peace. In the world ye shall have tribulation: but be of good cheer; I have overcome the world."

Hopefully, you will experience more pleasant than painful experiences in life. But our contentment, even our fulfillment comes from Jesus and our relationship with Him, not our circumstances.

Our prayer and hope is that whatever we go through, others will see Christ in us. Look at these painful experiences that Paul went through. In II Corinthians 11:23–28 KJV, he states:

> [23]*Are they ministers of Christ? (I speak as a fool) I am more; in labors more abundant, in stripes above measure, in prisons more frequent, in deaths oft.*

> [24]*Of the Jews five times received I forty stripes save one.*

> [25]*Thrice was I beaten with rods, once was I stoned, thrice I suffered shipwreck, a night and a day I have been in the deep;*

> [26]*In journeyings often, in perils of waters, in perils of robbers, in perils by mine own countrymen, in perils by the heathen, in perils in the city, in perils in the wilderness, in perils in the sea, in perils among false brethren;*

27In weariness and painfulness, in watchings often, in hunger and thirst, in fastings often, in cold and nakedness.

28Beside those things that are without, that which cometh upon me daily, the care of all the churches.

In II Corinthians 12:10, he repeated his contentment premise again with "Therefore I take pleasure in infirmities, in reproaches, in necessities, in persecutions, in distresses for Christ's sake: for when I am weak, then am I strong" (KJV).

Paul taught and lived that whatever I experience, whatever challenge or circumstance I go through, Jesus must be seen and glorified in me. That's a good place to stop, reread, and pray. That is Christian maturity. That is total surrender. That is Kingdom living!

If you are experiencing painful circumstances in your life—ask the Lord to speak peace not into your storm, but into you and for the Lord to teach you to be content in all of life's circumstances. You say, "I struggle." That's okay. Read this verse again. Paul said he had to "learn" to be content. Be patient—keep trusting—and you'll get there.

Philippians 4:11 "Not that I speak in respect of want: for I have learned, in whatsoever state I am, therewith to be content."

Yes, you can be content!

CHAPTER 12

I CAN BE FLEXIBLE

I know how to be abased, and I know how to abound. Everywhere and in all things I have learned both to be full and to be hungry, both to abound and to suffer need.

Philippians 4:12 (NKJV)

This attitude, this characteristic, this trait is so needed in the Christian world today. Yes, be dogmatic in your core values, beliefs, doctrines, and principles; but in preferences, opinions, personal ideas, like and dislikes—be flexible.

Many years ago, when Edgewood was located on Railroad Street in Blue Mountain, I visited the neighbor next door to the church. He was very elderly, couldn't see well, and didn't keep a clean house. My friends know that I have a problem with nastiness. We sat on a dirty couch that had no real cushions, so when I sat down, my seat went to the ground.

He wanted to show me pictures of his family, so he got a box from his cabinets, sat down next to me, and opened the box. Dozens of roaches ran out. Because of bad eyesight, he never saw them—but I did! Needless to say, we visited. I attempted to share Christ, invite him to church, prayed with him, then left, after 30–40 minutes of visiting. I'll never forget that dirty and difficult visit.

Later that day, I was asked to go see a Mr. Weaver at a local hospital. I went and met him, talked to him, and in passing, I asked him where he lived. He told me to look out the window. He said, "Do you see that house on the hill?"

I replied. "The one with the five pillars in front?"

He said, "Yes, that's my house." Wow—mansion was more like it! We prayed for his healing, and I left thinking that in the same day, I have visited a man as poor as Joe's turkey, and I visited a very, very wealthy man.

I felt good knowing that I could minister to whomever God sent me. It didn't matter whether it was those on welfare or those who had wealth.

I've had the privilege to preach camps where some have been in bad condition and others were like five-star hotels. I've been on mission trips where we stayed in jungles and eaten rodents and monkeys. I've been on Alaskan cruises where we had steak and lobster. I have seen and experienced unbelievable sights. I've dealt with saints and sinners. It doesn't matter—we must be flexible, adjustable, and adaptable.

Paul said in I Corinthians 9:22, "I am made all things to all men that I might by all means save some." Paul teaches us with his life and his words to be flexible.

The issues in church that we get hung up on are so often style and preferences, music, governmental structure, colors, arrangements, etc. We must be flexible, or we will win the battle and lose the war with our Christian brothers and sisters. Again, never compromise your convictions, but there are a lot of issues where it just doesn't matter.

Probably the biggest issue in the church in the last ten to twenty years is the change in the type of music used in worship. People like certain styles, have preferences, and get very upset when their style of music is not played or sung. Churches bicker, Christians argue, and His Kingdom suffers because believers are not flexible! We must learn this principle in our walk with God: "I can be flexible."

Now, I'm not teaching compromising your conviction or giving slippery grace! No, No! But with a lot of preferences—let it go. Be flexible. Show grace. The principle of being flexible is very important in relationships with people. You will not always agree with people, but you can get along with them.

It seems to be a pattern for believers that the older we get, and the longer we walk with Christ, the less flexible we become. We do need to be dogmatic in Bible doctrine, and strong and stable in our principles and core values. But when it comes to preferences, personal taste, likes and dislikes, let it go. Matter of fact, Paul states in Philippians 2:4, "Look not every man to his own things (interests), but every man also on the things (interests) of others." Look out for their interests—what they think, what they like, what they want. Give up your rights and wants. That's spiritual maturity.

Why should I be flexible?

1. To reach the lost. You "become all things to all people so that by all means people will be saved" (I Corinthians 9:22).

2. To bless other believers. Matthew 5:9 says, "Blessed are the peacemakers, for they are the children of God."

3. To keep your joy. Some people are so stubborn that they get messed up and mess up other people with their hard-headedness. "Rebellion is as sinful as witchcraft and stubbornness as bad as worshiping idols. So because you have rejected

the command of the Lord, He has rejected you as king" (I Samuel 15:23).

4. To keep you from getting needlessly hurt. Remember, it's not about me—it's about Him and others! Consider this short poem, "Epitaph on Mike O'Day's Tombstone."

> "This is the grave of Mike O'Day, who died maintaining his right of way. His right was clear, his will was strong. Now he's just as dead as if he'd been wrong."

5. To keep good priorities. You don't major in minors. Don't make mountains out of molehills.

6. To keep the focus on Jesus—not yourself. That is the key! Matthew 22:37 tells us: Jesus replied, "you must love the Lord your God with all your heart, all your soul, and your entire mind."

You will not always agree with people, but you can be flexible and show them respect and show them the love of Christ. Dale Carnegie calls it "letting them save face."

Philippians 4:12 says, "I know both how to be abased, and I know how to abound: everywhere and in all things, I am instructed both to be full and to be hungry, both to abound and to suffer need."

Yes, you can be flexible!

CHAPTER 13

I CAN DO THIS!

I can do all things through Christ who strengthens me.

Philippians 4:13 (NKJV)

We land on verse 13 like a plane landing on a long runway. Paul has said all of this in verses 1–12 to say this in verse 13. "I can do *all things* through Christ who strengthens me." His conclusion is that no matter what he goes through, endures, has set before him, that with Jesus' help he can do anything! That's the right attitude and spirit.

Here's what we have learned: we choose our attitude. We are responsible for our attitude.

People say, "I can't control my attitude."

I say, "With God's help, yes you can!"

Here's an example. A couple will be arguing, and tempers will flare, and then the phone will ring, and one of them answers the phone in the kindest, nicest, sweetest voice and says, "Hello." They did it! Right there, they controlled their tempers and attitude. The passage tells me that it doesn't matter what you are going through. You can have the right attitude for that situation, whatever the situation . . . and that takes the Lord's strength.

> *The old story goes that one day a farmer's donkey fell into a well. The animal cried for hours as the farmer tried to figure out what to do.*

> *Finally, he decided the animal was old, and the well needed to be covered up anyway; it just wasn't worth it to retrieve the donkey.*

He invited all his neighbors to come over and help him. They all grabbed a shovel and began to shovel dirt into the well. At first, the donkey realized what was happening and cried horribly. Then, to everyone's amazement, he quieted down.

A few shovel loads later, the farmer finally looked down the well. He was astonished at what he saw. With each shovel of dirt that hit his back, the donkey was doing something amazing. He would shake it off and step up onto the dirt the people had put into the well.

As the farmer's neighbors continued to shovel dirt on top of the animal, he would shake it off and take a step up.

Pretty soon, everyone was amazed as the donkey stepped up over the edge of the well and trotted off!

Life is going to shovel dirt on you—all kinds of dirt. The key to getting out of the well is to shake it off and take a step up. Each of our troubles is a stepping-stone. We can get out of the deepest wells not by stopping but by stepping up. That's the right attitude. Shake it off and take a step up.

We choose our attitude. I remember being in a men's prayer group on Sunday morning and saying, "Let's pray for a good day." Then a good brother of mine said, "It *is* a good day."

I realized right then and there how right he was! It's David Livingston's attitude (that great missionary to Africa) who said, "I love life and I'll go anywhere as long as it's forward."

Charles Swindoll wrote years ago in his book *Attitudes, the Power of a Positive Outlook*:

> *"The longer I live, the more I realize the impact of attitude on my life. Attitude to me is more important than facts. It is more important than the past, than education, than money, than circumstances, than failures, than successes, than what other people think or say or do. It is more important than appearance, talent or skill. It will make or break a company…a church…a home. The remarkable thing is that we have a choice everyday regarding the attitude we will embrace for that day. We cannot change our past…we cannot change the fact that people will act in a certain way. We cannot change the inevitable. The only thing we can do is play on the string we have, and that is our attitude. I am convinced that life is 10% what happens to me and 90% how I react to it. And so it is with you…we are in charge of our attitudes."*

When our girls were in school, we noticed that most parents were always concerned and emphasizing the "aptitude" part of education. And we should be concerned because it is important. But Myra and I were far more concerned about the "attitude" part of our girls' lives. Things like respect for elders and teachers, trying and doing your best, caring for and helping others. We believed right attitude in life will take you farther than knowledge, high IQ, or aptitude.

Dale Carnegie says, "Students with A's and B's will come back to the school and be the teachers. The students with B's and

C's will come back and be the principal." It's the attitude, not the aptitude.

We know that your attitude will determine most of your life. We've all seen and experienced people with a bad attitude. You can spot or even feel them a mile away. They're no fun to be around. On the other hand, the person with the great attitude—they are a blessing to be around! So, choose a great attitude, pray about your attitude, and work daily on your attitude.

I love the little prayer of the person who prayed, "Lord, so far today I've been nice and kind. I haven't raised my voice to anybody or said anything bad . . . but in a few minutes, I'm gonna get out of bed, and I'm really gonna need your help." The truth is, we really do need His help!

We spend thirty minutes to an hour every morning getting ready for work, school, or life; primping, washing, cleaning, and preparing outwardly for the day. If we'd invest thirty minutes to an hour every day in God's Word and prayer, reading, memorizing, meditating, growing, developing a Christ-like spirit and attitude, we would be much better off in life and be much closer to the Lord.

Paul is saying in this chapter. Yes, you can! With the Holy Spirit in your life, you have a power that the world doesn't have.

A family had been in church, and the preacher preached about Jonah and the great fish and how Jonah spent three days and nights in the belly of that large fish. In the car on the way home, the little boy looked at his dad and said, "I don't think I believe that Jonah lived in the fish for three days."

The dad paused then and asked, "Do you believe that God created man?"

The little boy said, "Yes, sir." The dad then asked. "Do you believe that God created fish?" The little boy said, "Yes, sir."

Then the dad said, "Well, then, couldn't God make a fish that would house a man for three days?"

The little boy paused, thought about it for a minute, and said, "Well, if you're gonna bring God into it, that changes everything!" And it does!

God can change everything, and he can change you. You can become an "I can!" Christian. An overcomer. An anything is possible believer. How do I know? Read Philippians 4:13 again, and you'll see it in a totally different light.

Philippians 4:13, tells us, "I can do all things through Christ which strengtheneth me" (KJV). Look closely:

> *I can*—tells us Paul had an attitude to succeed.—He was an "I Can" man

> *I can do*—Tells us he had a commitment and was willing to put forth much effort to succeed.

I can do all things—Tells us Paul knew and
understood that with God's spirit and power
that all things are possible.

I can do all things through Christ—Tells us Paul
knew where his strength and power to
succeed came from.

*I can do all things through Christ who strengthens
me*—Tells us Paul understands that it is not
self-confidence that is the key to success,
but rather God-confidence that gives us the
power and strength to become a confident,
positive, and overcoming Christian.

So my friend, "yes, you can!"

A quick review:

- 4:1 You can love others.

- 4:2 You can be a peacemaker.

- 4:3 You can help.

- 4:4 You can rejoice.

- 4:5 You can be disciplined.

- 4:6 You can pray.

- 4:7 You can have peace.

- 4:8 You can think right.

- 4:9 You can do right.

- 4:10 You can be thankful.

- 4:11 You can be content.

- 4:12 You can be flexible.

- 4:13 You can do all things!

Let me sum it all up with a favorite acrostic of mine from Philippians 4:13. Take those first two words of that verse and write them vertically. Make an acrostic out of them.

I CAN...

I stands for Imagine! Imagine the person God wants you to be.

C stands for Commit! Commit yourself to being the person God wants you to be.

A stands for Affirm it daily. That is—daily do the things God would have you to do to be who He wants you to be.

N stands for Never! Never, never, never give up!

Always strive to be who God wants you to be. You say, "Preacher, what if I fail?" Then get forgiveness, and pick up right where you left off. Here's what I know: "Yes, you can!"

The bottom line—you can do anything through Christ, who strengthens you.

Matter of fact, Philippians 4:13 says, "I can do *all things* through Christ who strengthens me."

Yes, you can!
God said you can!

CHAPTER 14

CONCLUSION

Now to Him who is able to do exceedingly abundantly above all that we ask or think, according to the power that works in us,

Ephesians 3:20 (NKJV)

In our study, we have learned we are equipped to defeat the devil and to live a victorious Christian life. I close with my favorite "life" passage. We see in Ephesians 3:20 KJV, "Now unto him that is able to do exceeding abundantly above all that we ask or think, according to the power that worketh in us,…"

The NLT puts it this way: "Now all glory to God, who is able, through his mighty power at work within us, to accomplish infinitely more than we might ask or think."

This certainly is an "I can" verse. Look at how it reads and what it tells us. It opens up all kinds of possibilities, potential, and probabilities. It tells us what we already know: that God can do so very much more than we can think, imagine, or ask.

1. If we have a 30-voice choir, I can pray and ask God to fill the choir, give us new choir members, and help the choir to grow to 100. To this God says, "You think and ask too small. I can do exceedingly abundantly more."

2. If we have 30 teens in our youth program, and we'd like to grow and reach more teens and reach 100 in the group, we pray for that and God says, "You think and ask too small. I can do exceedingly abundantly more."

3. You can do the same with the children's ministry.

4. You can do the same about souls and church growth.

That's ministry, but we could do the same with marriage and family, finances, fitness, and our future. The KJV uses the words "exceeding abundantly."

The NIV uses the words "immeasurably more."

The NLT uses the words "accomplish infinitively more."

God can do far more than we can ever imagine, dream, guess, or request.

In the Greek language, these two words "exceeding abundantly" are actually three Greek words packed into one word. Literally it is "uperekparasos." Let's break it down. 1. uper 2. ek 3. parasos. Parasos means perfect. The way it should be—normal—right.

Ek means out of. Over, more.

Uper means super. Grand, glorious (like Superbowl).

For example: If you have a creek in your yard, most of the time, it will be within its normal banks. The water flows down the creek the way it normally does. That's parasos—normal. If it rains a lot, perhaps the water level rises and reaches the banks of the river and splashes over a little. That's Ek-Parasos—out of; over. Every once in a while, it rains for days and days. The water level in that creek rises, and rises, and rises—over the banks and into the yard and surrounding areas until it floods the place. That's uperekparasos.

God is saying in Ephesians 3:20 that He wants to *flood* our lives with blessings, and grace and favor, but it's "according to the power that works in us." He can do much more than we think or imagine. We are the ones "to limit" or "to allow" God working in our lives. He did a work for us (salvation), to do a work through us (ministry).

**If you are in a trial,
you might be saying,
"I can't make it."**

**God says,
"You can not only make it;
you are an overcomer!"**

**You say,
"I can't live this Christian life."**

**God says,
"You can not only live it,
but you can also live a holy life."**

**You say,
"I can't serve."**

**God says,
"Yes, you can!"**

My prayer is that God would flood your life with His presence, power, and peace. The message is this: With God's help—with His Holy Spirit in you—you can do *all* things! Don't let anyone come into your life and limit you. You have potential. Your life is before you. God believes in you. I do, too!

Believe God. Allow Him to work in you and through you no matter what the issue. No matter how big or how difficult it is, God can come into your life and "uperekparasos" you!

He is a big God with wonderful plans for your life.

Ephesians 3:20 says Yes—God can.

ABOUT THE AUTHOR

DR. BILL SNOW

Dr. Bill Snow serves as senior pastor of Edgewood Congregational Methodist Church in Anniston, Alabama. He has served there for thirty-six years, and has seen the church grow, relocate, renovate, purchase property, add staff, complete a second phase and become a very holy, healthy, and happy church.

He is married to Myra, his sweetheart, for more than forty years. Their two grown daughters are married. Matt and April Martin have two wonderful children, Elijah and Hosanna Martin. Brandon and Autumn Grammer have two wonderful children, Elly and Kayden Grammer.

Dr. Snow received his Bachelor of Arts degree from Wesley College in 1984. Later, he received his Masters and Doctorate degrees from Covington Theological Seminary where he graduated Magna Cum Laude. Pastor Bill enjoys sports, competition, family, and serving the Lord.

Made in the USA
Columbia, SC
31 December 2021